"NOTHING EXISTS ALONE..."
— Rachel Carson

*To my nature-loving mom,
Marie-Luise Roth
—With love, SRS*

Springdale, Pennsylvania

SPRING AFTER SPRING

How Rachel Carson INSPIRED the Environmental Movement

Stephanie Roth Sisson

ROARING BROOK PRESS

New York

It was dawn when the
chorus began.

Rachel didn't want to miss a note.

And wonders big . . .

and small.

Spring was Rachel's favorite time of year.

As the sun set, she could hear the first bubbles of frogsong.
Crickets began their nighttime tune and bats squeaked a lullaby.

At home there was a warm supper and a big family. Mom played the piano, and Dad sang songs and read stories.

Rachel's favorites were those about the sea.

As the days grew longer and warmer, the chattering, chirping, and hooting got louder.

Until the gathering calls from migrating birds meant that it was autumn. They were coming together for their long journey through the ocean of air to their wintering homes.

But not everyone left.

Snuggled under a warm blanket, Rachel drew pictures and wrote about the life she experienced all year.

She read books about animals and imagined what their lives were like.

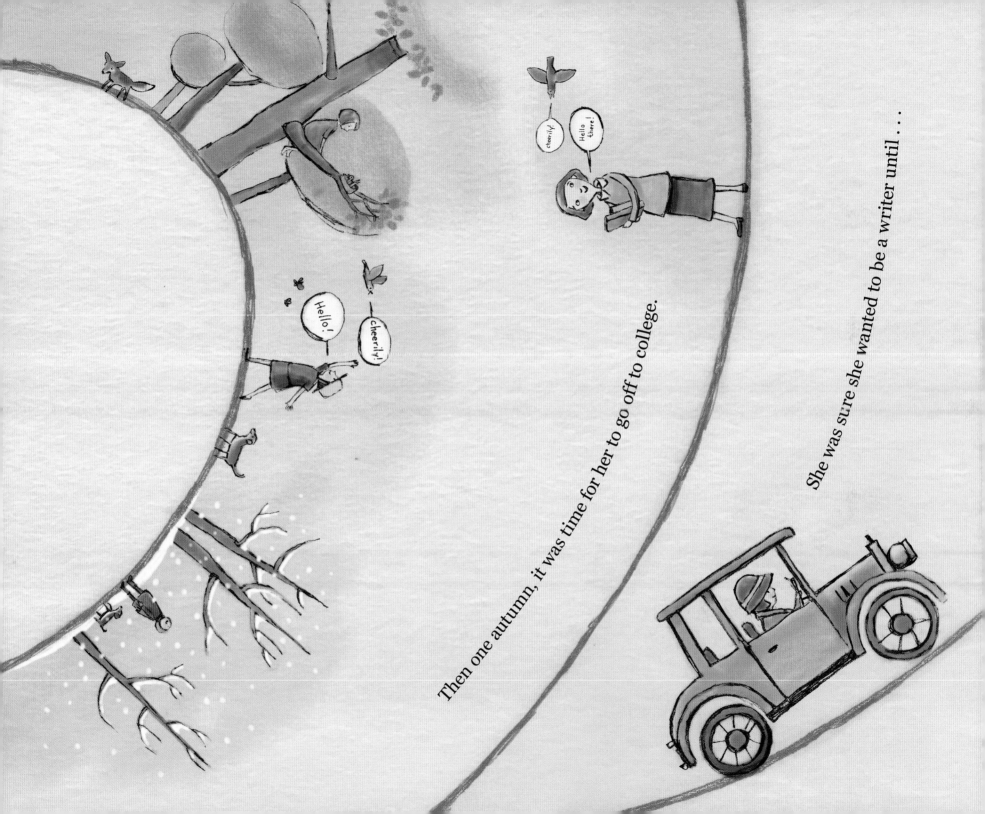

Then one autumn, it was time for her to go off to college.

She was sure she wanted to be a writer until . . .

. . . she looked through a microscope and saw a small world in a drop of water—tiny sea plants and animals. Rachel was amazed and in love.

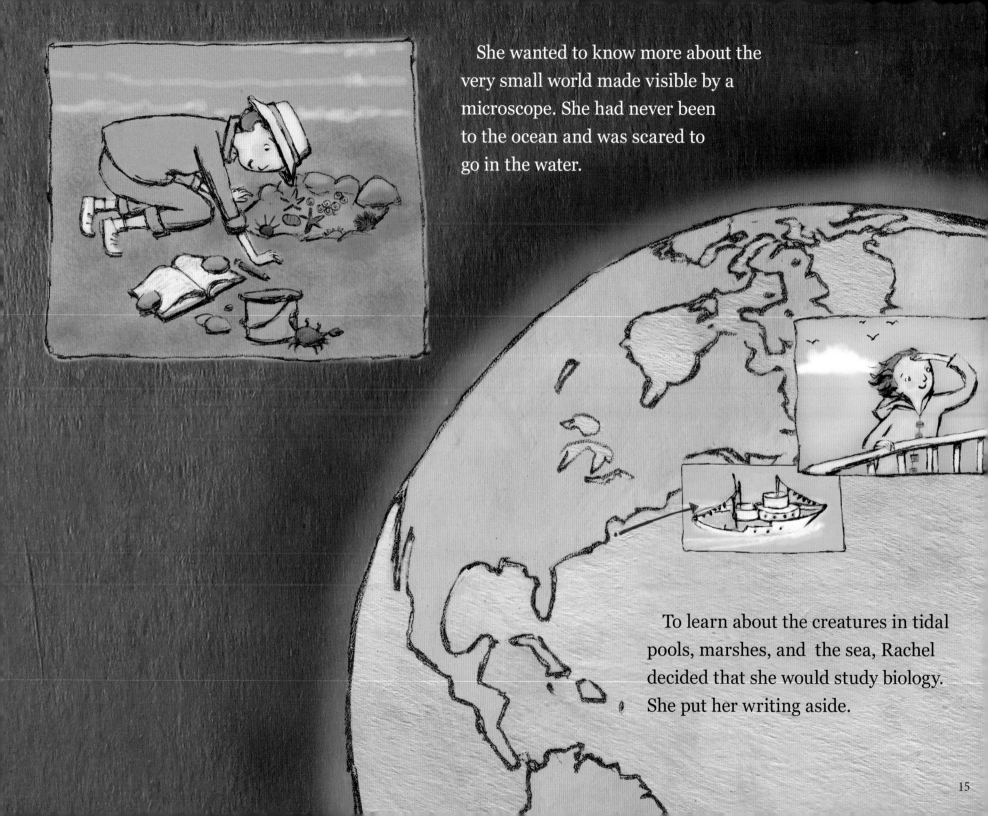

She wanted to know more about the very small world made visible by a microscope. She had never been to the ocean and was scared to go in the water.

To learn about the creatures in tidal pools, marshes, and the sea, Rachel decided that she would study biology. She put her writing aside.

After she finished school, Rachel worked as a scientist and compiled information about the ocean. Now for her job she wanted to know what it was like to actually be underwater. She was still scared. But she went anyway.

IN THE FISH WORLD, MANY THINGS ARE TOLD BY SOUND WAVES...."

Rachel began to write books about the sea. They were so full of scientific detail and vivid descriptions of the lives of sea creatures that people could imagine those worlds.

Rachel became a famous author.

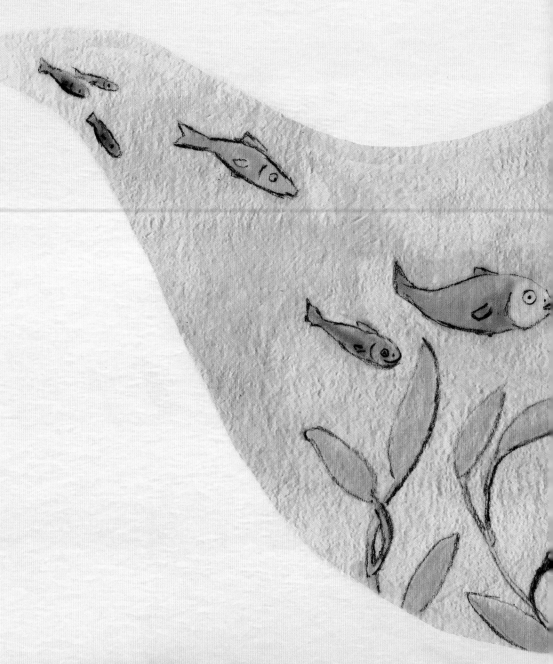

Under the Sea *Wind*

The Island lay in shadows only a little deeper than those that were swiftly stealing

But there was
something wrong.

All around, nature's voices were going quiet.

So Rachel did what she did best: she watched closely, listened carefully, and learned as much as she could about what was happening.

Rachel put together scattered facts and found the answer.

People wanted to kill bugs that ate their plants, bothered them, and sometimes even made them sick.

Chemists created new poisons to solve the insect problems that *seemed* to work and *seemed* to be harmless to other creatures and humans.

These poisonous chemicals were quickly used everywhere in huge amounts because people thought they were safe.

But Rachel found evidence that the poisons were not safe.

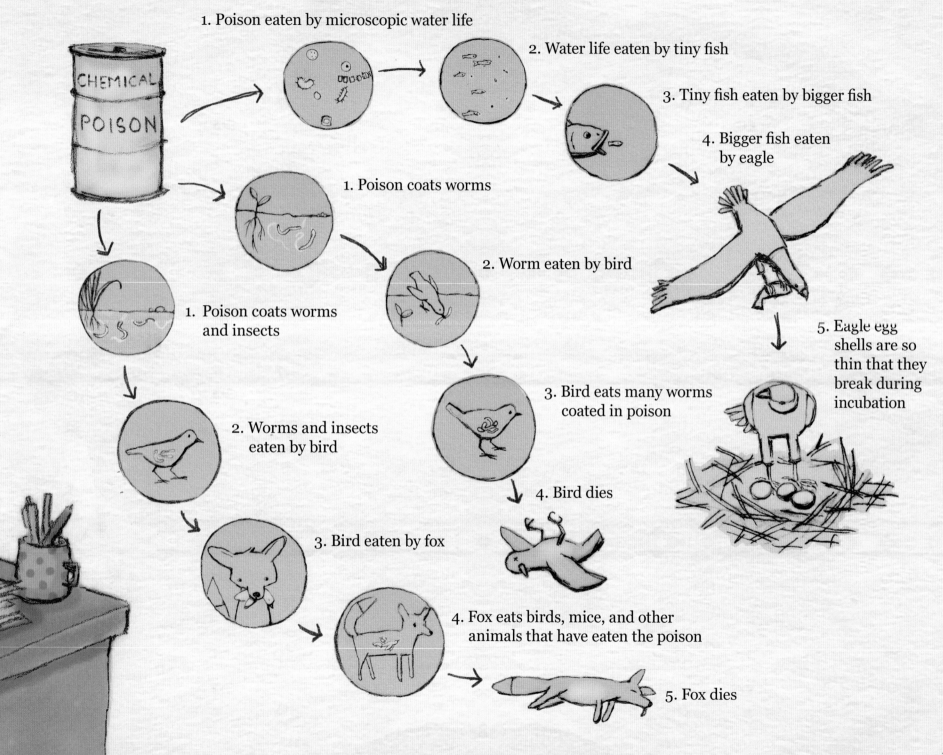

1. Poison eaten by microscopic water life

2. Water life eaten by tiny fish

3. Tiny fish eaten by bigger fish

4. Bigger fish eaten by eagle

1. Poison coats worms

2. Worm eaten by bird

3. Bird eats many worms coated in poison

5. Eagle egg shells are so thin that they break during incubation

1. Poison coats worms and insects

2. Worms and insects eaten by bird

3. Bird eaten by fox

4. Bird dies

4. Fox eats birds, mice, and other animals that have eaten the poison

5. Fox dies

Rachel wrote a book to tell people what she had learned.

Silent Spring created a huge ruckus. Some people were inspired to change, but many didn't believe Rachel.

Eventually President Kennedy took notice and began an investigation to find out what was true. Rachel was asked to come to Washington, D.C., and defend her book.

She was scared,
but she went.

Rachel's testimony in Washington and her writing in *Silent Spring* made people see that they have an effect on the environment and the other creatures that they share the world with.

People were inspired to speak up, congress passed new laws so that nature was treated with more care, and some of the most harmful chemicals were banned.

Spring after spring, year after year, people celebrated the Earth and the environment because Rachel showed them how beautiful and precious it is.

27

But Rachel went home and continued watching and listening. In the morning, she went out among the tide pools and gathered specimens. In the afternoon, she carefully studied them and took notes on her observations. And in the evening, when the tide had gone out again, she returned each creature with great care—exactly in the spot she had found it.

Exactly where it belonged.

I have long loved Rachel Carson's writing, especially her books about the wonders of nature where she writes so poetically about science. But her most famous book, *Silent Spring*, is hard for me to read because it's a warning about what happens when people are not careful.

Silent Spring is one of those rare books that changes the way a whole society thinks. In the 1950s, people thought that science could solve all their problems and that nature could be controlled through chemicals—no one questioned that. Except Rachel Carson. In a 1963 television interview, Rachel said, "the balance of nature is built on a series of relationships between living things and their environment." Rachel knew chemicals had their place. But she asked people to slow down and look carefully at what they were doing and to understand that by affecting the tiniest creature, they were influencing the whole web of life, including humans. In the end, I realized that *Silent Spring* is about ecology and the wonders of nature, just like all her other books. And I came to love it as well.

Rachel died on April 14, 1964, just two years after writing *Silent Spring*. She was fifty-seven years old. She never saw the full impact of her work. *Silent Spring* led to the formation of the Environmental Protection Agency, it inspired people to try to find less harmful ways to deal with pests, and it is widely seen as the beginning of the environmental movement, which led to the creation of Earth Day. Rachel Carson gave a voice to nature and an awareness of peoples' connection to our fragile planet. However, pesticides and herbicides are still used in large quantities all over the world, and they still negatively effect many animal species as well as humans. There is still much to learn about the relationship between living things and their environment, and this knowledge is crucial to understanding climate change.

Today, Rachel's writing is as important as ever.

NOTES

Front endpapers: Rachel Carson said that her love of nature was inherited from her mother who had a "love of all living things."

Title page: Springdale, Pennsylvania, sits in a bend of the Allegheny River. When Rachel was growing up, her family's farmstead was like an island in a sea of forests and streams. Just beyond the Carson homestead were a steel factory, a glass factory, an aluminum factory, as well as coal mining and iron smelting and other industries—all of which created smells and put particles into the air. Rachel was always aware of how people endangered nature.

1: Dawn is the best time of day to hear birds because they are staking out their territory, finding mates, and calling out messages to one another. It is mostly the male birds that do the singing. Birds continue singing all through the day, but the dawn is the most intense.

2–3: At the beginning of the twentieth century, there was an educational movement that encouraged the careful observation and understanding of nature. Rachel's mother had been a school teacher, and she made the outdoors Rachel's classroom. Rachel spent much of her childhood exploring the woodlands and streams around her family's homestead with her dog, Candy.

4–5: Insects have to wait until the air warms up to make sounds because the body parts they use to make sound need heat to move well.

7: Rachel was the youngest child in her family. Rachel's homelife was not always easy, but in the good times the Carsons took turns reading poems and stories. Rachel's favorite song was "Rocked in the Cradle of the Deep," and when she got older, her favorite poem was Alfred Tennyson's "Locksely Hall." She had a fascination with the sea even though she lived nowhere near it, nor had she ever seen it. She later said, "Even as a child—long before I had ever seen it—I used to imagine what it would look like, and what the surf sounded like."

9: Rachel was a good student and kept up with her school work even though her mother often kept her home from school when various illnesses like scarlet fever (which was often fatal) were going around or if the skies were particularly polluted with smoke and soot from nearby factories, making it difficult to breathe.

11: Beatrix Potter's books were Rachel's favorites, along with *The Wind in the Willows* by Kenneth Grahame. She loved books about nature.

12–13: At age eleven Rachel sent a story to *St. Nicholas Magazine* and became a published author. Other writers who began their careers at the magazine include E. B. White, E. E. Cummings, and F. Scott Fitzgerald. "I can remember no time, even in earliest childhood, when I didn't assume I was going to be a writer . . . I read a great deal almost from infancy, and I suppose I must have realized someone wrote the books." The Carsons valued education, and when it was time for Rachel to go to college, the family put their homestead up as collateral for a loan for Rachel to complete her studies.

14–15: At first, Rachel was an English major at Chatham University (then called the Pennsylvania College for Women), but after taking a class in biology from her teacher, Mary Scott Skinker, who made the subject come alive for Rachel, she changed her major from English to biology.

16–17: Rachel continued on with her studies at Woods Hole Oceanographic Institute. She earned a masters degree in zoology from Johns Hopkins.

18: Rachel was hired as junior aquatic biologist at the U.S. Bureau of Fisheries. Her job involved analyzing research and writing pamphlets. When her boss, Mr. Higgins, saw her writing, he thought it was too good for just pamphlets and suggested she send it in to the *Atlantic* magazine. She wrote a series of articles that would eventually become the beginnings of her first book, *Under the Sea-Wind* (1941). That was followed by *The Sea Around Us* (1950), which won the National Book Award, and *The Edge of the Sea* (1955). All of her books eventually became bestsellers.

19: During World War II (1939–1945), new chemicals that had been created in laboratories were used to kill pest insects and weeds. Because Rachel was a scientist and worked at the Bureau of Fisheries (later the Bureau of Fisheries and Wildlife), she read research on these new chemicals and began to be concerned about their effects on life.

20–21: All over the world, the chemicals that had been created for the war were being put into products and applied widely on land, in water, and in homes and neighborhoods. No one thought they were dangerous. In 1958, Rachel received a letter from her friend Olga Owens Huckins about an aerial spraying of chemical pesticides on her land. Many dead and dying birds were found afterward. Reports like her friend's were written about in newspapers, usually on the back pages, but still the chemicals continued to be used without limit.

22–23: Rachel had been aware of the dangers of pesticides and herbicides since just after the World War II, through her job at the Bureau of Fisheries. Many reports had come across her desk over the years describing the unintended consequences they were having. Rachel wrote to E. B. White, the editor of the *New Yorker*, and suggested he write a series of articles about the effects of chemicals in the natural world. E. B. White suggested that she write them herself. The project eventually became *Silent Spring*.

24–25: Rachel felt it was important to share the facts she knew so that people could make informed choices. *Silent Spring* gave them that knowledge. The companies that made the chemicals were not pleased and tried to discredit Rachel. But the public outcry was so loud that the government listened and further studied the problems with the chemicals.

26–27: As a result of *Silent Spring*, the government set out to protect people and wild life from the overuse of potentially dangerous chemicals. Rachel Carson's legacy was to share her love of living things and her deep understanding of the world we are all a part of.

Back endpapers: Rachel loved sharing nature's wonders with her adopted son, Roger Christie, just as her mother had with her.

BIBLIOGRAPHY

Brooks, Paul. *Rachel Carson: The Author at Work*. San Francisco: Sierra Club Books, 1998.

Carson, Rachel. *Always, Rachel: the Letters of Rachel Carson and Dorothy Freeman 1952–1964: The Story of a Remarkable Friendship*. Edited by Martha Freeman. Boston: Beacon Press, 1994.

Carson, Rachel. *The Edge of the Sea*. Boston: Houghton Mifflin, 1955.

Carson, Rachel. *The Lost Woods: The Discovered Writing of Rachel Carson*. Edited by Linda Lear. Boston: Beacon Press, 1998.

Carson, Rachel. *The Sea Around Us*. London: Staples Press Limited, 1951.

Carson, Rachel. *The Sense of Wonder*. New York: Harper & Row, Publishers, Inc., 1965.

Carson, Rachel. *Silent Spring*. Boston: Houghton Mifflin, 1962.

Carson, Rachel. *Under the Sea-Wind*. New York: Penguin Group, 1996.

Goodwin, Neil (writer & producer). *American Experience: Rachel Carson's Silent Spring*. WGBH Boston Video, 1993.

Lear, Linda. *Rachel Carson: Witness for Nature*. New York: Henry Holt and Company, 1997.

McMullen, Jay (writer & producer). *The Silent Spring of Rachel Carson*. CBS Reports, April 3 1963, Season 4, Episode 14.

Payton, Brian. "Rachel Carson (1907–1964)." NASA Earth Observatory. earthobservatory.nasa.gov/Features/Carson/Carson2.php.

Wolff, Daniel. *How Lincoln Learned to Read: Twelve Great Americans and the Educations That Made Them*. New York: Bloomsbury, 2009.

SOURCE NOTES

Front endpapers "In nature, nothing exists alone." Carson, Rachel, *Silent Spring*.

17 "In the fish world, many things are told by sound waves." Carson, Rachel. *The Edge of the Sea*.

29 "The balance of nature is built on a series of relationships between living things and their environment." McMullen, Jay, *The Silent Spring of Rachel Carson*.

30 "Love of all living things." Carson, Rachel, *Always, Rachel*.

30 "Even as a child . . . what the surf sounded like." Wolff, *How Lincoln Learned to Read*.

30 "I can remember no time, even in early infancy when I didn't assume I was going to be a writer . . ." Carson, Rachel. *The Lost Woods*.

Back endpapers "As human beings, we are part of the whole stream of life." Carson, Rachel, *The Lost Woods*.

A special thanks to my dear friend and great admirer of Rachel Carson, Sharon Lovejoy.

Also a big thank-you to Katherine Jacobs for her guidance and patience on this project.

Published by Roaring Brook Press
Roaring Brook Press is a division of Holtzbrinck
Publishing Holdings Limited Partnership
175 Fifth Avenue, New York, NY 10010
mackids.com

Library of Congress Control Number: 2017957301
ISBN: 978-1-62672-819-6

Our books may be purchased in bulk for promotional, educational, or business use. Please contact your local bookseller or the Macmillan Corporate and Premium Sales Department at (800) 221-7945 ext. 5442 or by e-mail at MacmillanSpecialMarkets@macmillan.com.

First edition, 2018
Book design by Andrew Arnold
Printed in China by RR Donnelley Asia Printing Solutions Ltd., Dongguan City, Guangdong Province

3   5   7   9   10   8   6   4   2

"AS HUMAN BEINGS, WE ARE PART OF THE